W9-CBG-133

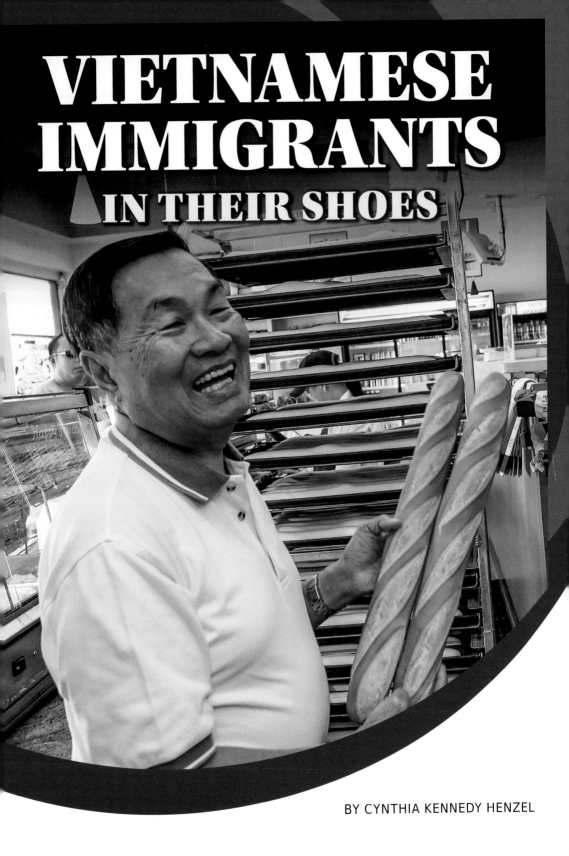

VIETNAMESE IMMIGRANTS
IN THEIR SHOES

BY CYNTHIA KENNEDY HENZEL

The Child's World®
childsworld.com

Published by The Child's World®
1980 Lookout Drive • Mankato, MN 56003-1705
800-599-READ • www.childsworld.com

Content Consultant: Thao L. Ha, PhD, Professor of Sociology, MiraCosta College

Photographs ©: Damian Dovarganes/AP Images, cover, 1, 26; AP Images, 6, 8, 12, 20; Department of Defense/AP Images, 11; Jeff Robbins/AP Images, 14; Red Line Editorial, 17; Eddie Adams/AP Images, 18; Elaine Thompson/AP Images, 23; Maika Elan/Bloomberg/Getty Images, 24; Lee Snider Photo Images/Shutterstock Images, 28

ISBN 9781503820326
LCCN 2016960932

Printed in the United States of America
PA02338

ABOUT THE AUTHOR

Cynthia Kennedy Henzel has a bachelor of science degree in social studies education and a master of science degree in geography. She has worked as a teacher-educator in many countries. Currently, she works writing books and developing education materials for social studies, science, and ELL students. She has written more than 80 books for young people.

TABLE OF CONTENTS

FAST FACTS

The First Wave of Vietnamese Immigration

- Immigration was triggered by the fall of South Vietnam to **Communist** North Vietnam.
- Most immigrants were high-ranking South Vietnamese officials or people who worked for Americans during the Vietnam War (1954–1975).
- They were assisted by the U.S. government and came quickly into the United States.

The Second Wave of Vietnamese Immigration

- Immigration was triggered by the release of prisoners from re-education camps. Others fled because of political or religious **persecution**.
- Most people fled by boat, going to **refugee** camps in southeast Asian countries.
- Many stayed in camps for months or years while waiting for a **sponsor** from the United States.

The Third Wave of Vietnamese Immigration

- Immigration was triggered by attempts to reunify families.
- Many were Amerasians (half American and half Vietnamese) who were persecuted in Vietnam.

TIMELINE

1954: Vietnam is split into North and South.

1954: More than 820,000 refugees flee from Communist North Vietnam to South Vietnam.

1965: The United States sends the first combat troops to defend South Vietnam.

1975: Saigon, the capital of South Vietnam, falls to North Vietnamese troops.

1975: The first wave of Vietnamese immigrants begins.

1978: The second wave of immigration begins, with many people fleeing Vietnam by boat.

1979: The United Nations begins the Orderly Departure Program to help Vietnamese immigrate to other countries safely.

1988: The U.S. Congress passes the Amerasian Homecoming Act, allowing Vietnamese children who have an American father and a Vietnamese mother to come to the United States.

2008: The last Vietnamese "boat people" begin arriving in the United States.

Chapter 1

THE FALL OF SAIGON

On April 28, 1975, Dzung Le and his family crammed into their car with their suitcases. Dzung's father drove to the spot where they would catch a bus to the airport. Shells exploded in the distance. People filled the streets. They were panicking as they tried to leave Saigon, the capital of South Vietnam.

The Vietnam War was drawing to a close, and the North Vietnamese army was advancing on the city. People in South Vietnam had reason to fear the invaders. In 1954, Communists had taken over the government of the North. Then they began a war to take over the South. The North's leaders were brutal, especially to the educated. Approximately 900,000 Vietnamese had fled from the North to the South.

The U.S. government did not want Communism to spread. So the U.S. military had supported the South Vietnamese government. But in 1975, with the war lost, the Americans were leaving the country. People who had worked for the Americans or for the South Vietnamese government feared they would be killed. For this reason, U.S. leaders had promised to **evacuate** South Vietnamese employees, their spouses, and their children younger than 16.

Dzung's father was a U.S. government employee, but Dzung Le was 18 years old. As the family waited for the bus, a soldier asked Dzung for his identification. "You are too old," the soldier said. "You're not 15."[1]

But Dzung insisted that he was 15 years old. Then Dzung's father showed the soldier Dzung's birth certificate. It was fake.

▲ **A U.S. helicopter takes off with Vietnamese refugees aboard.**

It said Dzung was younger than he really was. The soldier was still suspicious, but he let Dzung board the bus.

Dzung's family sat at the airport through the night as rockets fell. At dawn, they received bad news. Rockets had destroyed the runway. That meant no more planes could land.

Many people left the airport, joining the chaos in the streets of Saigon. Some people simply went home. Thousands of others went to the American Embassy and tried to push their way in.

They hoped the Americans would protect them and help them leave the country. Others lined the river trying to escape by boat.

A friend of Dzung's father, an American, told the family to stay at the airport. Helicopters were coming, but everyone had to leave their suitcases behind. A few hours later, Dzung heard a roar in the sky. A fleet of helicopters landed, and men with guns jumped out. They were U.S. Marines. They loaded nearly 50 people onto a helicopter meant to carry only ten people. As Dzung scrambled aboard with four of his sisters, he looked back. Soldiers held back his parents and other sister. The helicopter was full.

"I just sat there silently trying to swallow every moment. . . . The city was so beautiful, but I knew I'd never see it again."

—Nho Nguyen describing his helicopter flight out of Saigon[2]

An hour later, the helicopter landed on a U.S. aircraft carrier off the coast of Vietnam. The passengers held on to a rope as a soldier led them across the slick deck of the ship. Dzung finally collapsed when he made it to his bunk. Later arrivals would sleep on bubble wrap on the floor.

Another ship took the refugees to the U.S. territory of Guam. Approximately 111,000 refugees would eventually pass through this island. Dzung had little more than his clothes. He didn't know what had happened to the rest of his family. He thought he might never see them again.

As Saigon fell to the North Vietnamese, approximately 6,000 people left by air. They joined the more than 130,000 who had evacuated by air or boat during the last month.

Luckily, Dzung found the rest of his family in Guam. They flew to Camp Pendleton in California. As the family left the plane, a nurse poked them with a needle to **vaccinate** them. People gave them a few supplies, including extra clothes and toothbrushes. Dzung shivered in the cool air. Soldiers handed out military jackets. The adult-sized jackets hung below the children's knees.

Soldiers at Camp Pendleton had built tent cities for the refugees. More than 50,000 refugees came through Camp Pendleton. Dzung and his family had to wait for a sponsor. This volunteer would help them find a house and job in their new country. The children took classes to learn English and help them understand American culture. A few months later, a sponsor helped them rent a house and buy a car. Dzung's father couldn't find a job at first. Dzung and a sister worked to support the family.

Dzung began school at a community college. In time, he went to medical school and became a doctor in San Diego, California. "I feel that we are very lucky to be here, but there's 40 million at that time that weren't so lucky," he said. "It really hurts when you think about your close friends."[3]

▲ Vietnamese citizens crowd aboard a U.S. ship as they wait to be transferred to refugee camps.

Chapter 2

THE BOAT PEOPLE

Binh Tran was a soldier in the South Vietnamese army. He spoke English, so he was an interpreter for U.S. soldiers during the Vietnam War. When the last U.S. soldiers left, Tran got a job with the U.S. government. But Tran was not able to leave the country when the North took over Saigon. Like thousands of others who worked for the Americans, Tran received a letter from the new Communist government.

The letter told him to report to a re-education camp for ten days. There he would learn about the new government.

When Tran arrived, the Communists put him in jail. He had to leave his wife and three children behind. Tran and the other prisoners were forced to do hard work. They cut and peeled bamboo. They planted vegetables. Some built houses. With little food or shelter, many prisoners died in the camps.

After three years, Tran was released. However, he struggled to find a job. Many people had to sell their homes and possessions just to survive. Those who had money could bribe people in the government to let them escape the country. But that was very expensive. It cost more than $500 for a place on a boat. Those who made the journey came to be known as boat people.

Tran had little money, but his mother lived in the countryside and had a boat. So, in 1979, Tran went to visit her during the New Year holiday, thinking he would use her boat to escape. But he was caught before he arrived. Because he was traveling without permission, he was sent to jail for two weeks.

Tran waited another two years. His brother got a job as a teacher and moved to the countryside. The brother prepared a boat. In 1983, Tran was finally ready to attempt another escape.

He left in the middle of the night with his two sons and his brother. Tran felt heartbroken to leave behind his wife and daughter. But he was determined to see them again someday.

The four refugees set out in their tiny boat. Water washed over its sides. After four days, they landed on an American oil rig and were taken to a refugee camp in Malaysia.

At the camp, Tran often helped refugees communicate with U.S. officials. As a result, he began hearing their stories. Many people had fled in broken-down, overcrowded boats. These refugees did not know where they were going. This made it easy for pirates to take advantage of them. The pirates stole people's belongings and kidnapped girls. Approximately one-third of the boat people died at sea.

The Humanitarian Operation Program helped many Vietnamese citizens immigrate to the United States. So, after eight months, Tran was transferred to a camp in the Philippines. He waited another seven months, learning more English and taking classes about American culture. Finally, a church sponsored his family to come to the United States.

In 1984, Tran arrived in Holland, Michigan. He was with his two sons and his brother. The church rented a house for them.

◄ **Many Vietnamese citizens had to spend weeks aboard boats before they were allowed to enter refugee camps.**

> "At the camp, (the) U.S. delegation gave to us some information about a new place three days before our departure day. All we knew (was) cold—snow—north of America."
>
> *—Xuong Tran, a Vietnamese immigrant*[5]

However, it was hard to figure out this new country. They had to have health checks and fill out government forms. They couldn't find the foods they were familiar with. Meeting people was hard, and Tran missed his wife and daughter. But Tran slowly adjusted to life in the United States. "When we come over here, that means we have a chance to learn from two different cultures," Tran said. "We try to keep the good ones from my own culture. And I learn good ones from the new culture."[4]

Tran got a job as a security guard. He wanted to work in electronics as he had in Vietnam, but he didn't have any **documents** to show his education. Like many refugees, he had burned his documents out of fear that the North Vietnamese would discover his ties to the Americans.

Tran went back to school to study electronics. Every day for two years, he went to class after he was done with work.

He still couldn't get a job in technology, but he eventually made enough money to buy his own house.

In the next few years, more Vietnamese settled in Holland. Many brought their families. Tran had more friends, but he still missed his family. Then, in 1992, Tran was able to sponsor his wife and daughter to come to the United States. After nine years apart, the family was finally reunited.

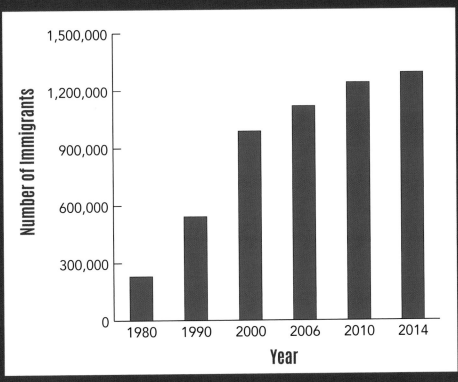

VIETNAMESE IMMIGRANTS IN THE UNITED STATES

Chapter 3

VIETNAMESE AND AMERICAN

In 1978, life was hard for nine-year-old Linh Quach and her family. Often, the main meal was watery rice. The family had no money. Then, the Communist government **drafted** Linh's 16-year-old sister into the army. Her parents knew the family had to escape. But all 12 of them could not go together.

In the middle of the night, Linh fled from Vietnam with her father and four of her siblings. As Linh joined more than 100 other refugees crammed onto a boat, she thought it was a great adventure. "It didn't hit me that we were leaving the country," she said.[6] But her older sister Chau cried and asked when she would see her mother again.

The boat was overloaded. To keep from sinking, the refugees threw extra food and clothing overboard. Hungry, thirsty, and often sick, they drifted for five days. Then a storm blew in. Large waves crashed over the boat's sides. They were sinking! Nearby oil rig workers pulled the last of the refugees off the boat as it disappeared into the ocean.

At a refugee camp in Malaysia, Linh's family was given lumber and plastic tarps. They used these materials to build a simple shelter. For four months, their father took them to the beach each day to look for her mother and sisters. Thousands of refugees arrived, but her family did not.

Linh's aunt, who had married an American man, sponsored the family. Linh and her family settled in Pennsylvania. Linh's two older sisters started working so that they could help support the family. Linh and two of her younger siblings started school.

Linh was surprised that no one else at the school spoke Vietnamese. "(On the) first day of school, I didn't realize it was me who had to change," she said.[7]

Then came bad news. After the family's escape, Linh's brother had died in Vietnam. Linh's father was devastated, but he continued trying to help his wife and daughters. In the early 1980s, he finally brought them from a refugee camp in the Philippines to the United States. After several years apart, Linh's mother barely recognized her.

Linh was part of a group known as the 1.5 **generation**. This generation is made up of immigrants who arrived in the United States as children and grew up with American culture. By the time Linh graduated from high school, she said she felt "very independent, very Americanized."[8]

Linh went to college. Meanwhile, her sister Chau began working with a charity that helped Amerasians. These were children born in Asia with American fathers and Asian mothers. In 1988, the U.S. Congress passed the Amerasian Homecoming Act. The act brought approximately 25,000 Amerasian children to the United States.

◄ **In Vietnam, Amerasian children were often looked down on by other Vietnamese citizens.**

Chau, like her sister, had adjusted to living in the United States. "I've kept a lot of Vietnamese traditions," she said. "But the very old-fashioned way—it's hard for me to live that way."[9]

Linh earned a degree in psychology in 1993 and planned to counsel children. Instead, she was offered a job as an interpreter with a charity to help new refugees. At first, Linh didn't want the job. She felt American, and working with refugees did not appeal to her. But she was good at the job. She was quickly promoted to help new refugees get resettled.

Linh settled into life as an American. In 1994, she went against tradition and married an American man from a German family. But she kept ties with her large family and the Vietnamese community. As she got older, she became more interested in her roots in Vietnam. She wanted to learn how to read and write in Vietnamese.

Linh was proud of her parents, especially her father. She said, "It's a big decision, risking his life to take us to Never-Never Land, hoping we'll have some opportunity wherever we end up."[10]

A teacher helps a Vietnamese American student learn the ▶ Vietnamese language.

Chapter 4

HELPING THOSE LEFT BEHIND

Binh Tran has the same name as his fellow immigrant in Michigan, but he had a very different experience. Tran was born in Vietnam, but he was part of the 1.5 generation. He came to the United States as a child in the 1970s. He grew up speaking English, and he went to American schools.

Like thousands of other Vietnamese children brought to the United States at a young age, he remembered nothing of his birth country.

Tran's family settled in California, and his mother worked hard to support her four children. At the time Tran was growing up, a technology boom was happening. His mother bought him a computer, and he soon developed software to chat with his friends. By the time he was a teenager, he had developed video games for Nintendo and PlayStation.

Tran went on to earn a degree in computer science at the University of California, Irvine. He worked for Microsoft after college, but he soon wanted to try developing his own ideas. He joined a small software company. Then he cofounded a company that helped schools manage special education programs.

In 2008, Tran and a business partner started a company called Klout. The company name came from the word *clout*, which means "influence." The company's software measured people's influence on social media. Klout gave people a score between 1 and 100. The score showed people's ability to drive ideas. The company grew, and in 2014 Tran and his partner sold it for $200 million.

PRODUCE OF U.S.A.

PRODUCE OF MEXICO

PLAIN PACK

RED GLOBE

BLACK SEEDLESS

BAG PACK

SON SEEDLESS

Tran, along with other successful Vietnamese **entrepreneurs**, started helping others succeed. He advised many new companies. Then, in 2014, Tran and Eddie Thai, a second-generation Vietnamese American, joined a company called 500 Startups. The company invests money in new companies in Vietnam. As Tran pointed out, "If you look at scores for Vietnam in reading, math and science, they actually score higher than countries like the U.S. and the U.K."[11]

Many people in the younger generations don't remember the struggles early Vietnamese immigrants faced. But strong family ties often keep them interested in their past. California has the largest Vietnamese community in the United States. The community is centered in Little Saigon, near Los Angeles. Many Vietnamese parents, like Tran's mother, teach their children the importance of education, family, and hard work. Little Saigon helps maintain these values.

Tran's relatives have all immigrated to the United States. "So," he said, "being able to come back (to Vietnam), to understand the people and get in touch with my roots, (while) at the same time, be a part of the foundation for Vietnam's future, that's an opportunity I just had to do."[12]

◄ **A Vietnamese American woman works in the Little Saigon area of Westminster, California.**

▲ **Vietnamese Americans take part in a parade in New York City.**

By 2014, nearly 1.3 million Vietnamese had immigrated to the United States. The values of family and respect for education have made many Vietnamese successful in the United States. Many have started businesses, particularly in the areas of technology, fishing, nail salons, and restaurants. Not all Vietnamese immigrants have been successful, but Vietnamese households today have higher-than-average incomes and lower-than-average poverty levels. Some of this may be due to having large households, which often include several generations.

By 2014, approximately 76 percent of Vietnamese immigrants in the United States had become citizens. This compares to 47 percent for all other immigrant groups. Many Vietnamese Americans maintain their language and culture by living in Vietnamese communities. They have used the opportunities and freedom in the United States to build better lives for themselves and their families. They have become Americans.

THINK ABOUT IT

- Why do you think many immigrants were willing to leave part of their family in Vietnam when they moved to the United States? What would you have done if you were in their situation?
- Vietnamese immigrants have settled in all 50 U.S. states. However, California and Texas are the states with the most Vietnamese immigrants. Why do you think those states became the most popular places for Vietnamese immigrants to settle?
- What do you think are the greatest challenges to a Vietnamese student starting school in the United States?

GLOSSARY

Communist (KAHM-yoo-nist): Communist means having to do with a system in which the government controls the economy. Many Vietnamese left the country to escape its Communist government.

drafted (DRAFT-ed): Drafted means forced someone to join the military. The Vietnamese government drafted people to fight in the war.

entrepreneurs (on-truh-preh-NOORZ): Entrepreneurs are people who start new businesses. Entrepreneurs are risk takers, because they may fail or succeed when starting a business.

evacuate (i-VAK-yoo-ate): Evacuate means to remove someone from a dangerous place. Many South Vietnamese citizens tried to evacuate before Saigon fell to the North Vietnamese.

generation (gen-er-AY-shun): A generation is a group of people born around the same time. First-generation immigrants grew up in Vietnam, but the 1.5 generation spent most of their childhood in the United States.

persecution (per-seh-KYOO-shun): Persecution is when people are treated unfairly or cruelly because of their beliefs. Many people fled Vietnam because they were facing political persecution.

refugee (ref-yoo-JEE): A refugee is a person who seeks safety in a foreign country, especially to avoid war or other dangers. The refugee fled Vietnam during the war.

sponsor (SPON-sur): A sponsor is a person who takes responsibility or pays for someone or something. Many immigrants cannot come to the United States unless they have a sponsor.

vaccinate (VAK-sin-ate): Vaccinate means to give someone a shot to avoid a disease. The nurse had to vaccinate the immigrants for measles.

SOURCE NOTES

1. Maureen Cavanaugh and Natalie Walsh. "Fall of Saigon Bittersweet for Vietnamese Refugee." *KPBS*. KPBS Public Broadcasting, 29 Apr. 2010. Web. 13 Dec. 2016.

2. Tom Berg. "Escape from Saigon: Find Out How These Refugees Fled as Their Homeland Fell 40 Years Ago Today." *Orange County Register*. Orange County Register & Digital First Media, 30 Apr. 2015. Web. 13 Dec. 2016.

3. Sharon Heilbrunn. "Vietnamese Refugee and Navy Veteran Reunite on the USS *Midway*." *KPBS*. KPBS Public Broadcasting, 29 Apr. 2010. Web. 13 Dec. 2016.

4. Donna M. Rottier. "Tran, Xuong Oral History Interview (Vietnamese): Asian and African American Residents of Holland." *Hope College Digital Commons*. Hope College, 7 July 1994. Web. 13 Dec. 2016.

5. Ibid.

6. Bob Batz, Jr. "Vietnam, 25 Years Later: Former Refugee Now Helps Others." *PG News*. PG Publishing, 24 Apr. 2000. Web. 13 Dec. 2016.

7. Ibid.

8. Ibid.

9. Kate Angell. "Stage Preview: 'Miss Saigon' Echoes Child Actor's Heritage." *PG News*. PG Publishing, 1 June 2003. Web. 13 Dec. 2016.

10. Bob Batz, Jr. "Vietnam, 25 Years Later: Former Refugee Now Helps Others." *PG News*. PG Publishing, 24 Apr. 2000. Web. 13 Dec. 2016.

11. Vivienne Nunis. "Could Vietnam Become the Next Silicon Valley?" *BBC News*. BBC, 2 Feb. 2016. Web. 13 Dec. 2016.

12. Ibid.

TO LEARN MORE

Books

Streissguth, Tom. *The Vietnam War*. Mankato, MN: The Child's World, 2015.

Willis, Terri. *Vietnam*. New York, NY: Children's Press, 2013.

Yasuda, Anita. *Vietnam*. New York, NY: AV2 by Weigl, 2017.

Web Sites

Visit our Web site for links about Vietnamese immigrants: childsworld.com/links

Note to Parents, Teachers, and Librarians: We routinely verify our Web links to make sure they are safe and active sites. So encourage your readers to check them out!

INDEX